THIS CANDLEWICK BOOK BELONGS TO:

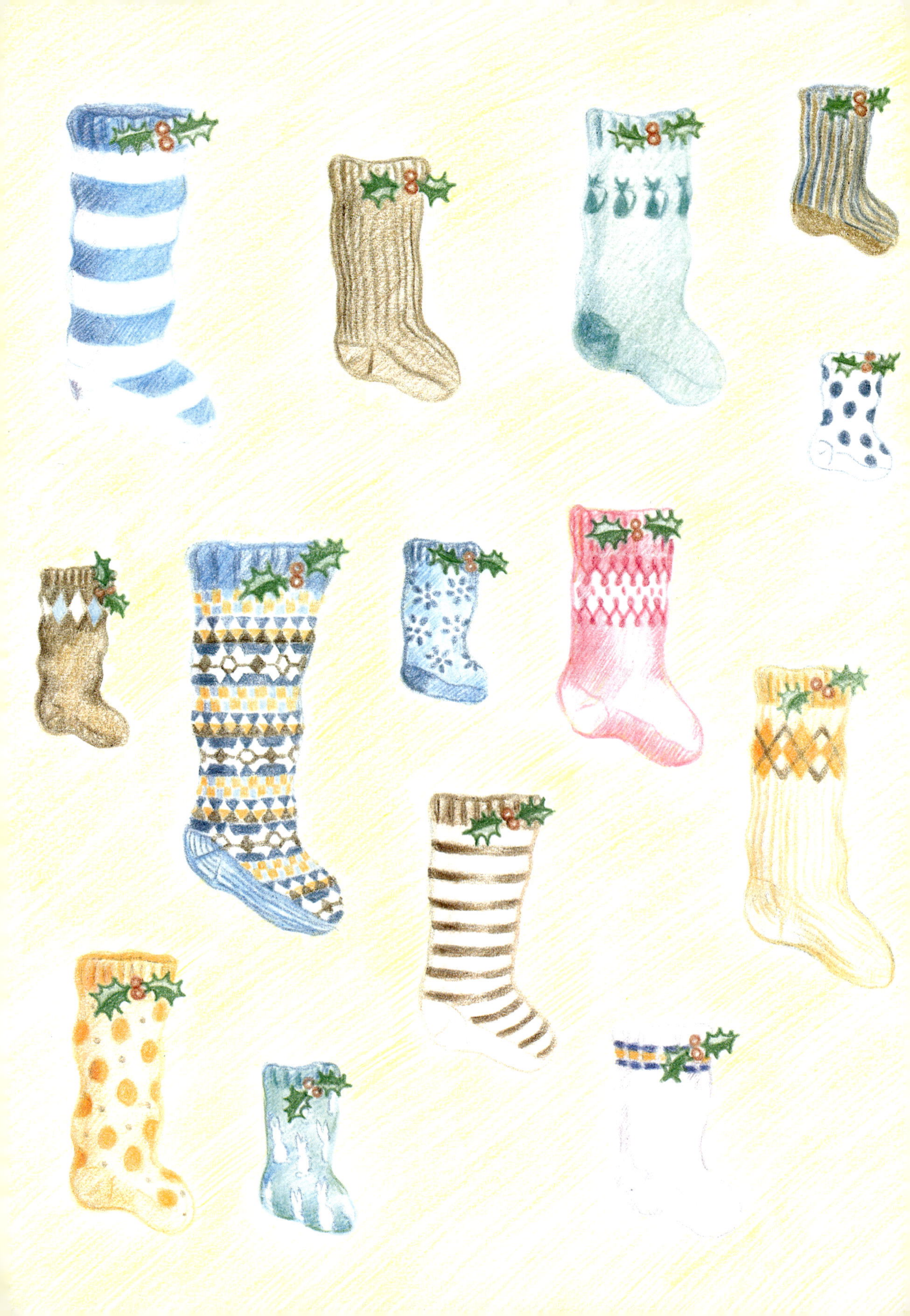

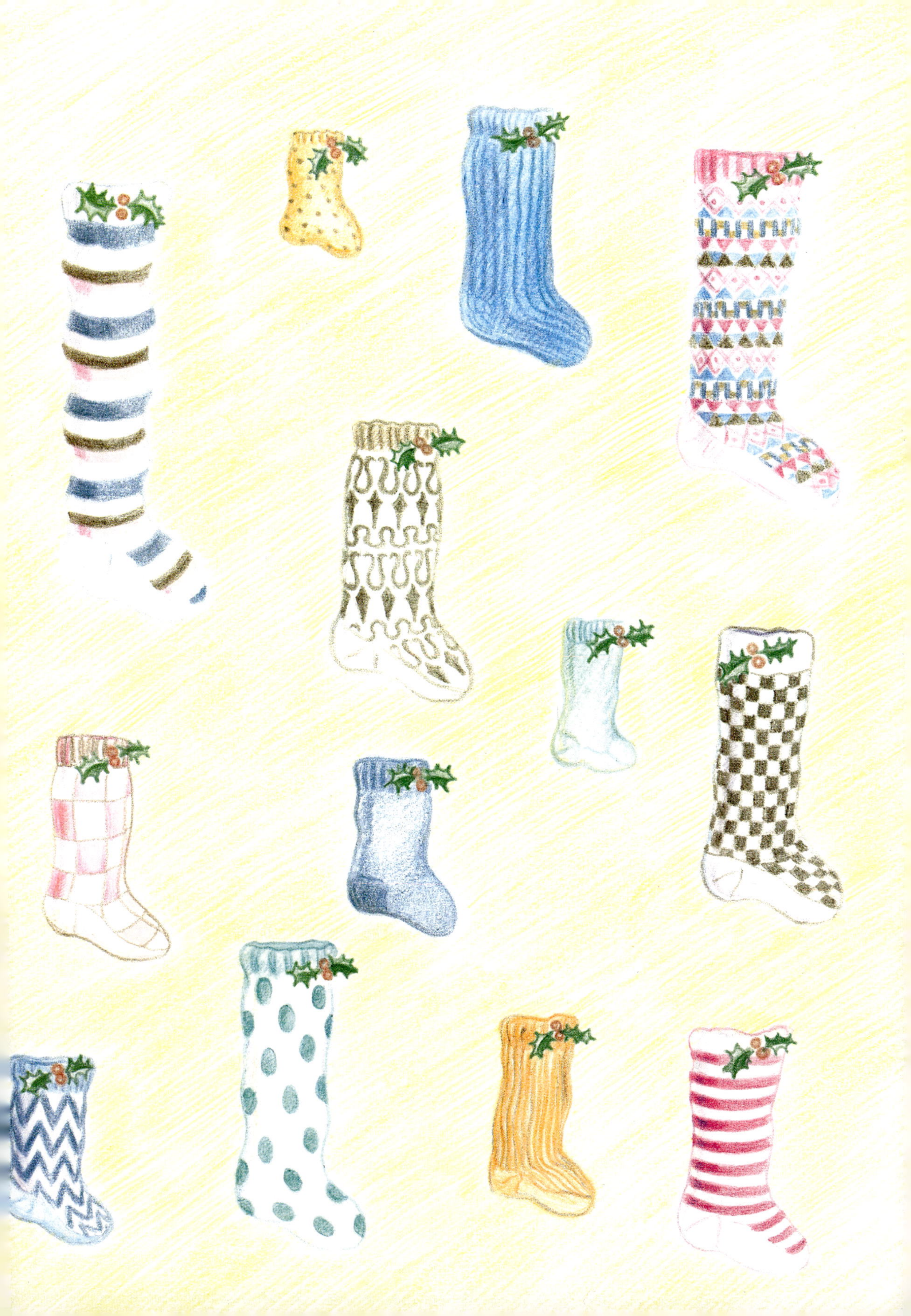

Illustrations copyright © 1989 by Lis Toft

All rights reserved.

Second U.S. paperback edition 1997

Library of Congress Catalog Card Number 95-67986

ISBN 0-7636-0351-1

2 4 6 8 10 9 7 5 3 1

Printed in Hong Kong

This book was typeset in Garamond Book.
The pictures were done in colored pencil.

Candlewick Press
2067 Massachusetts Avenue
Cambridge, Massachusetts 02140

The Night Before Christmas

Clement Clarke Moore

illustrated by Lis Toft

CANDLEWICK PRESS
CAMBRIDGE, MASSACHUSETTS

'Twas the night before Christmas, when
   all through the house
Not a creature was stirring, not even
   a mouse;
The stockings were hung by
   the chimney with care,
In hopes that St. Nicholas soon
   would be there;

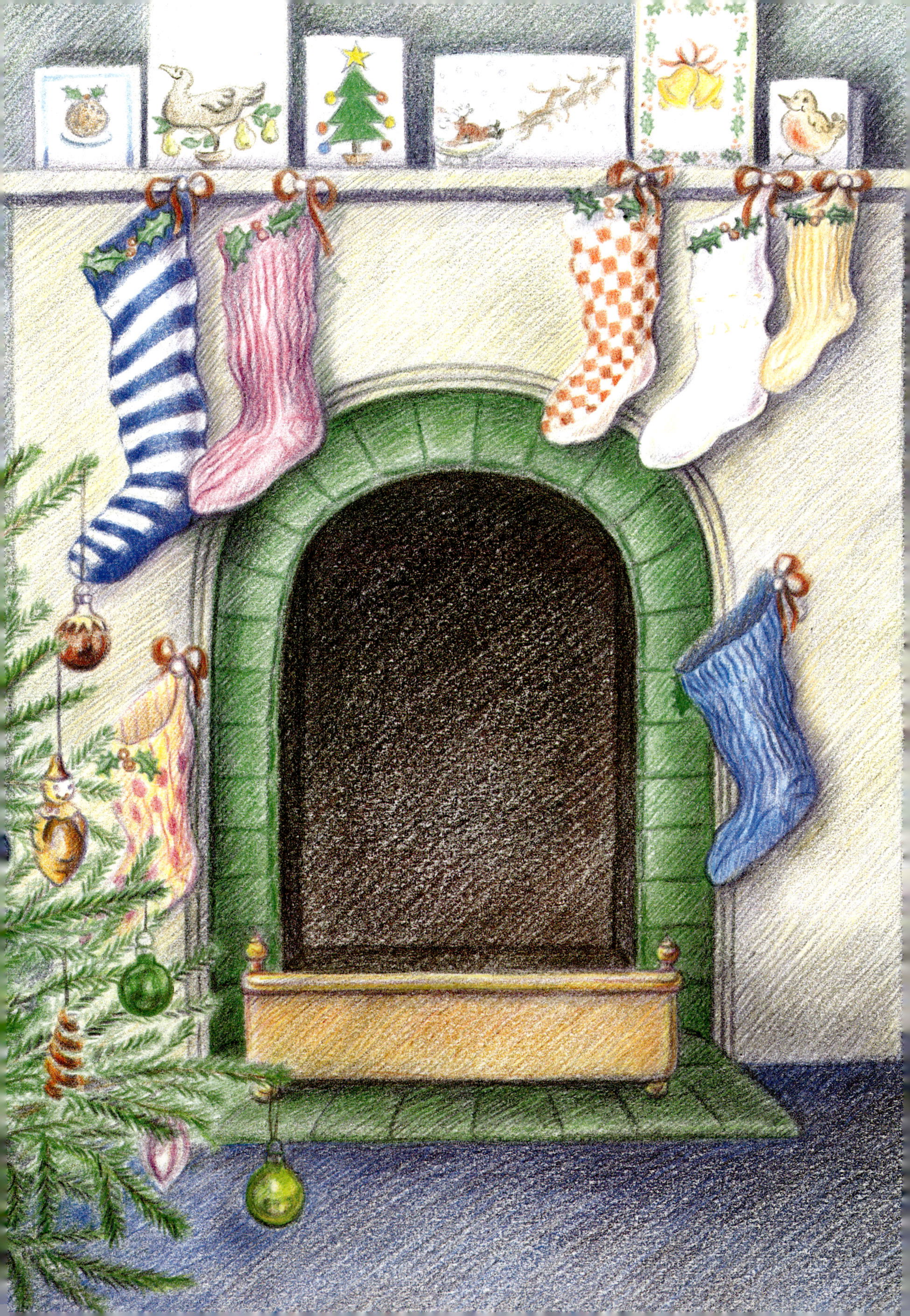

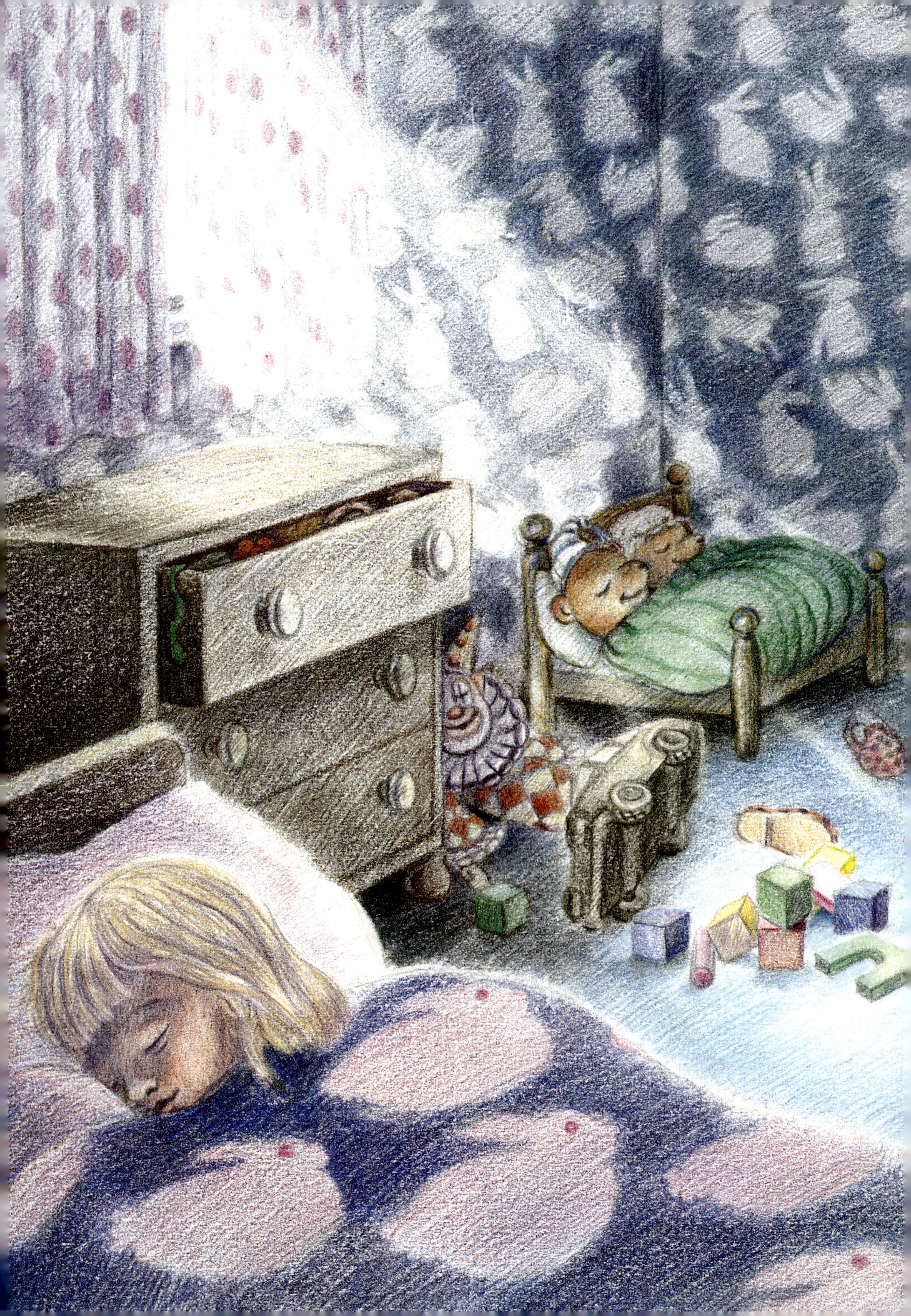

The children were nestled all snug in their beds,
While visions of sugar-plums danced in their
 heads;
And mamma in her kerchief, and I in my cap,
Had just settled our brains for a long
 winter nap—

When out on the lawn there arose such a clatter,
I sprang from my bed to see what was the matter.
Away to the window I flew like a flash,
Tore open the shutters and threw up the sash.

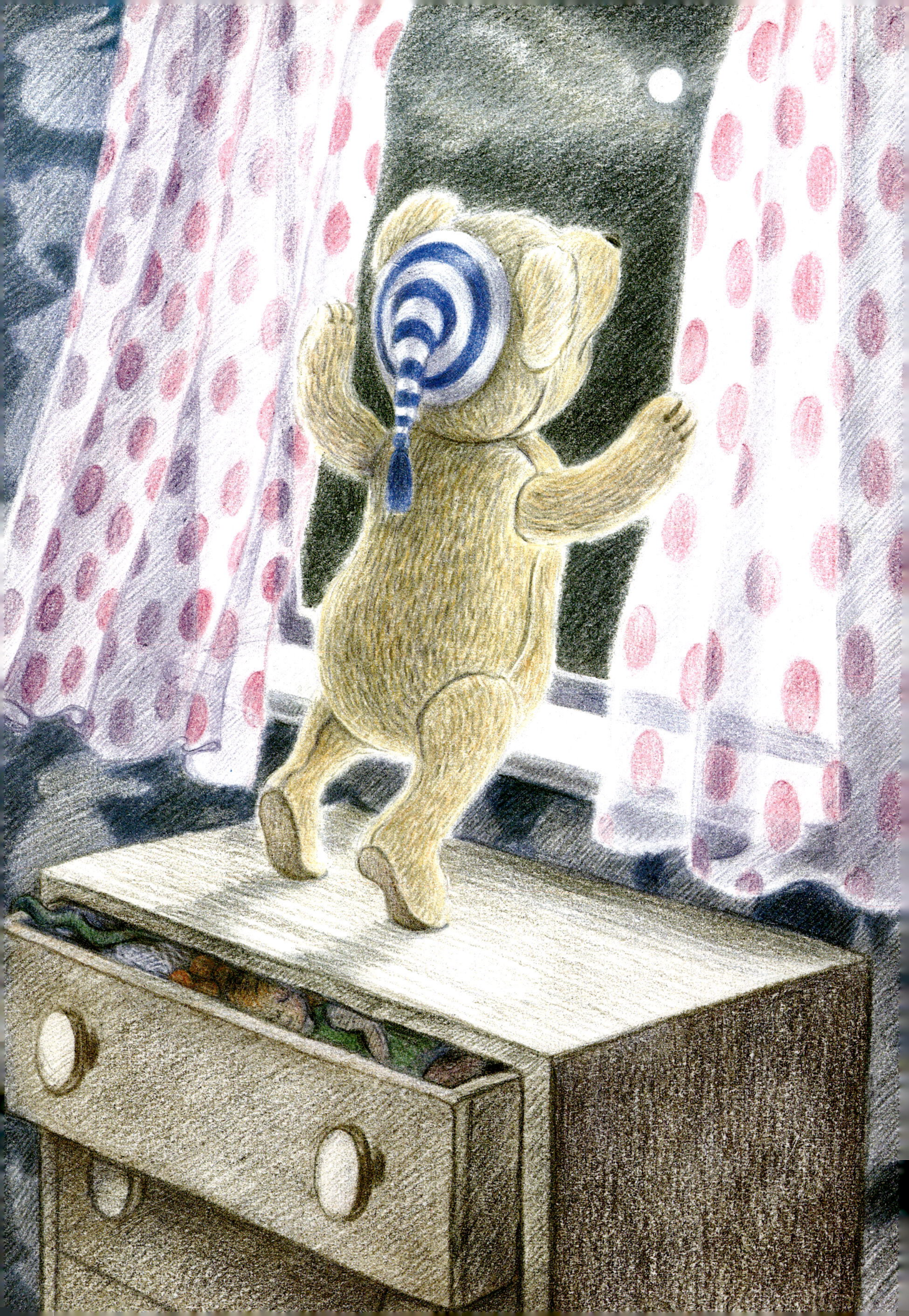

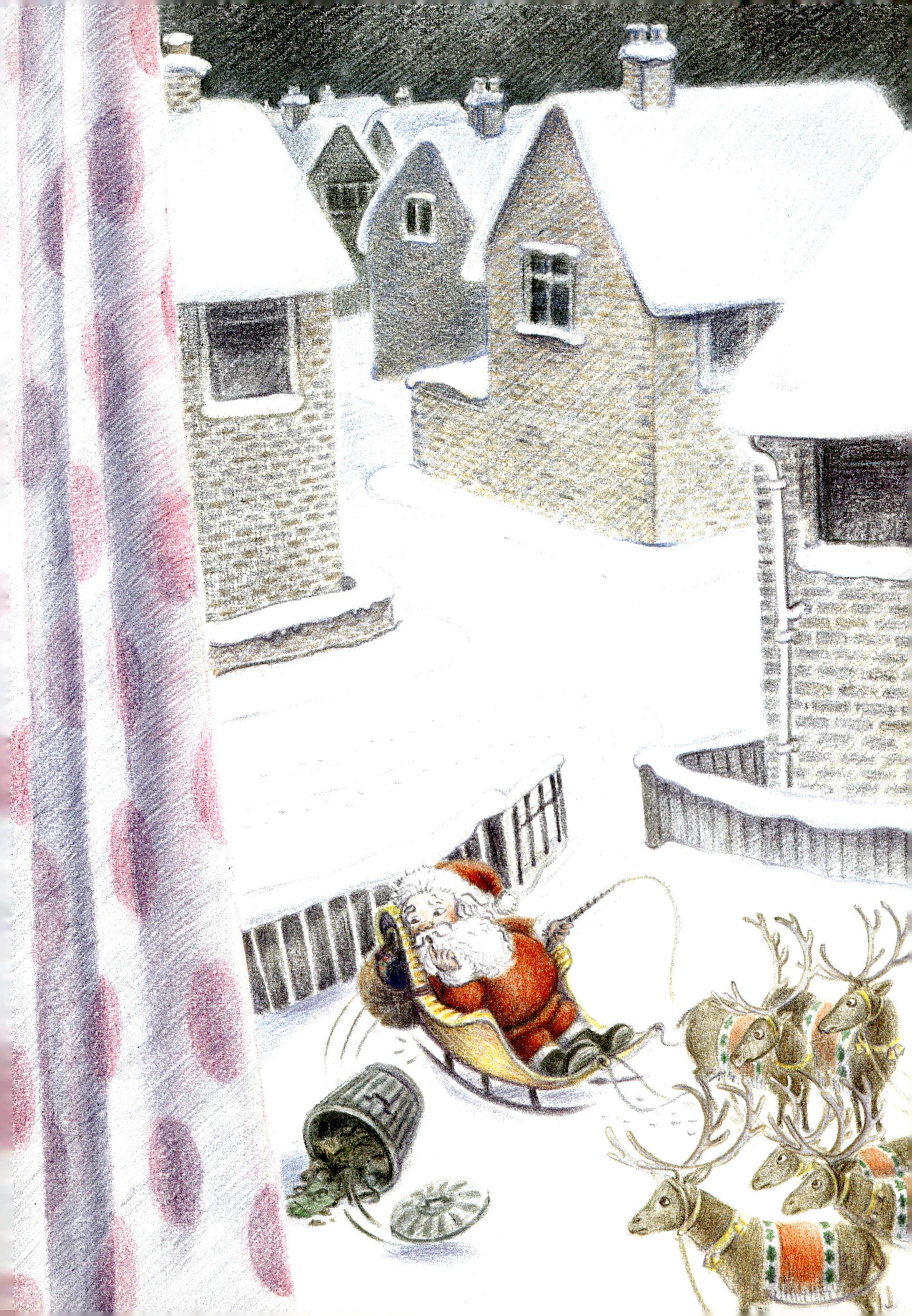

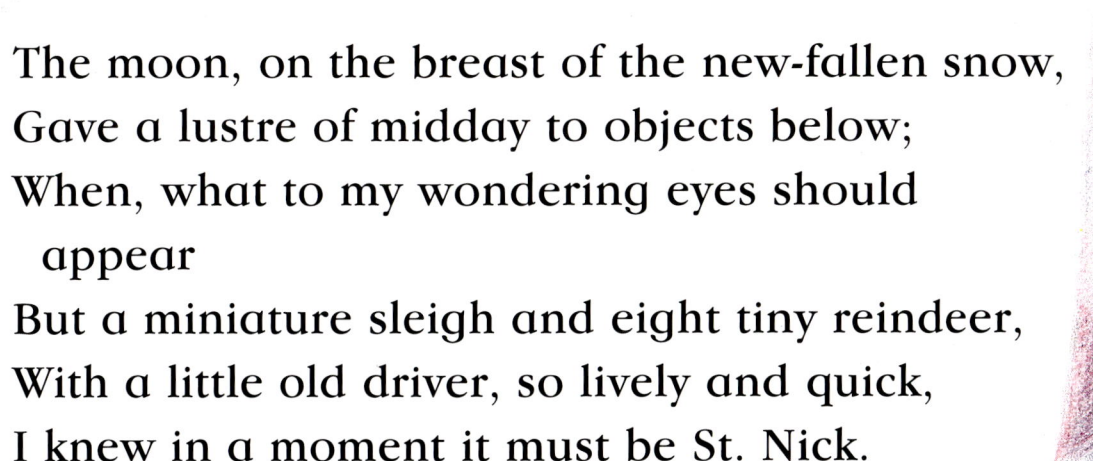

The moon, on the breast of the new-fallen snow,
Gave a lustre of midday to objects below;
When, what to my wondering eyes should appear
But a miniature sleigh and eight tiny reindeer,
With a little old driver, so lively and quick,
I knew in a moment it must be St. Nick.

More rapid than eagles his
  coursers they came,
And he whistled, and shouted, and
  called them by name:
"Now, Dasher! now, Dancer! now, Prancer
  and Vixen!
On, Comet! on, Cupid! on, Donder and Blitzen!
To the top of the porch, to the top of the wall!
Now, dash away, dash away, dash away all!"

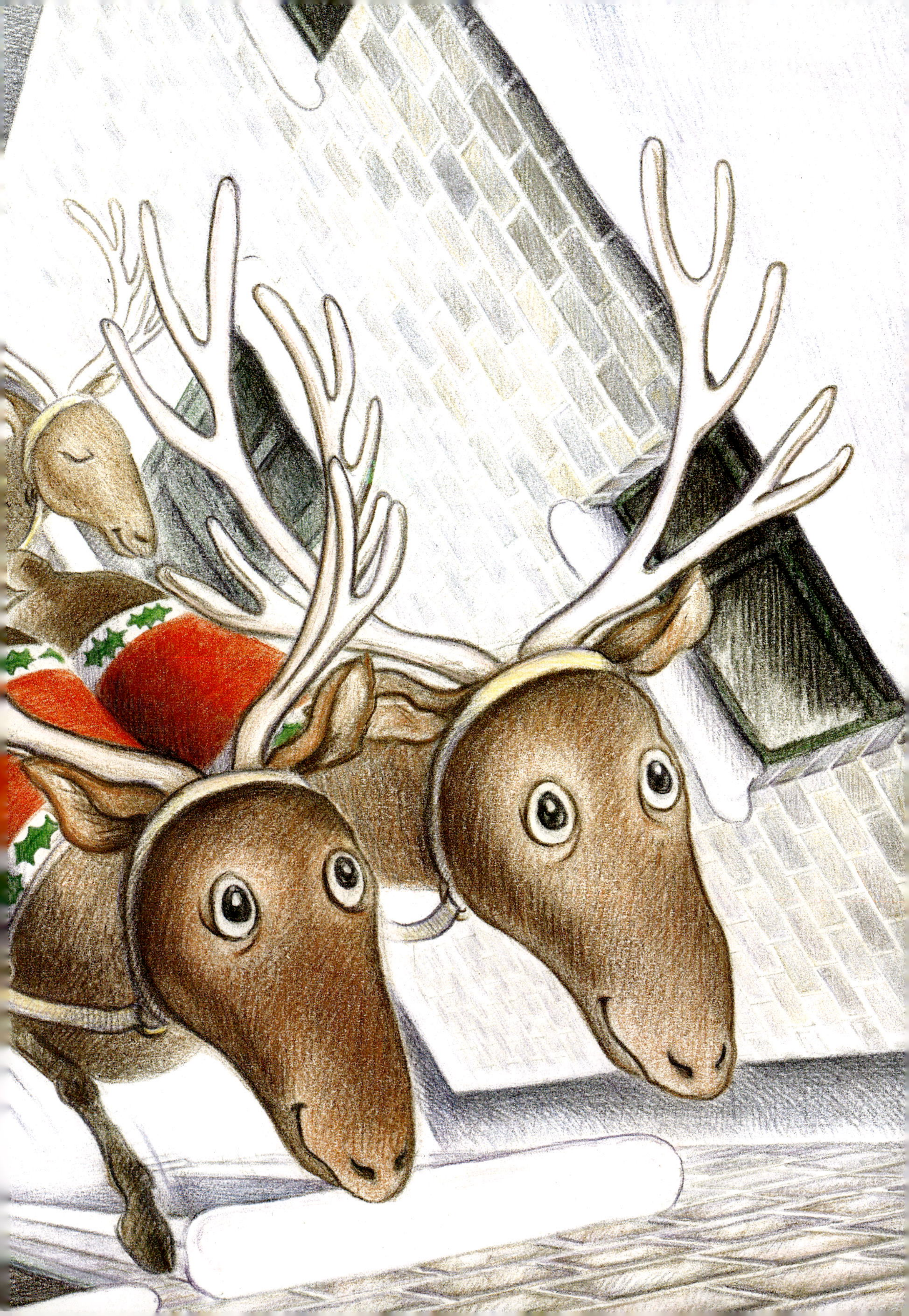

As dry leaves that before the wild hurricane fly,
When they meet with an obstacle, mount to
 the sky,
So up to the house-top the coursers
 they flew,
With the sleigh full of toys—and
 St. Nicholas too.

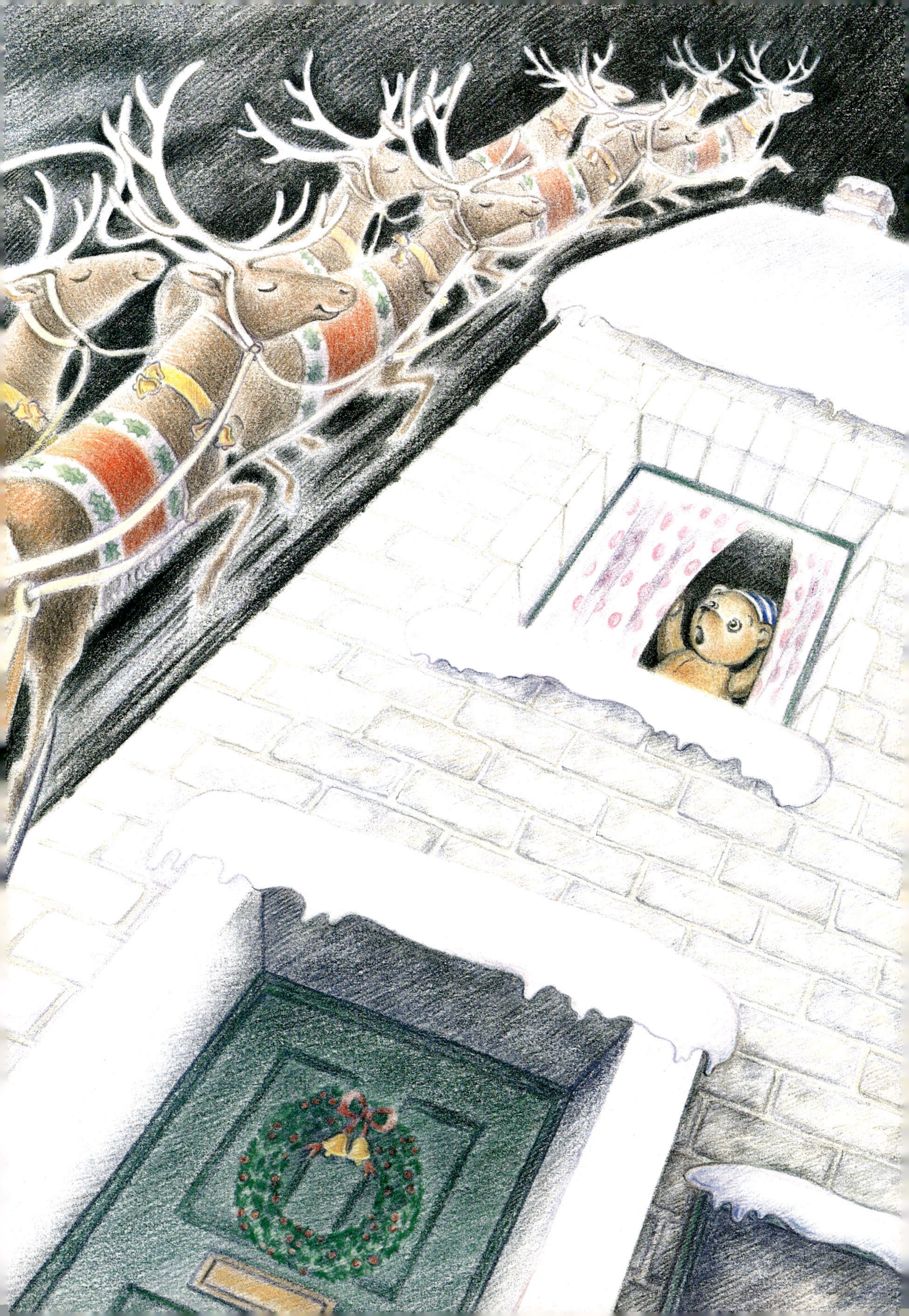

And then in a twinkling I heard on the roof
The prancing and pawing of each little hoof.
As I drew in my head, and was turning around,
Down the chimney St. Nicholas came with a bound.

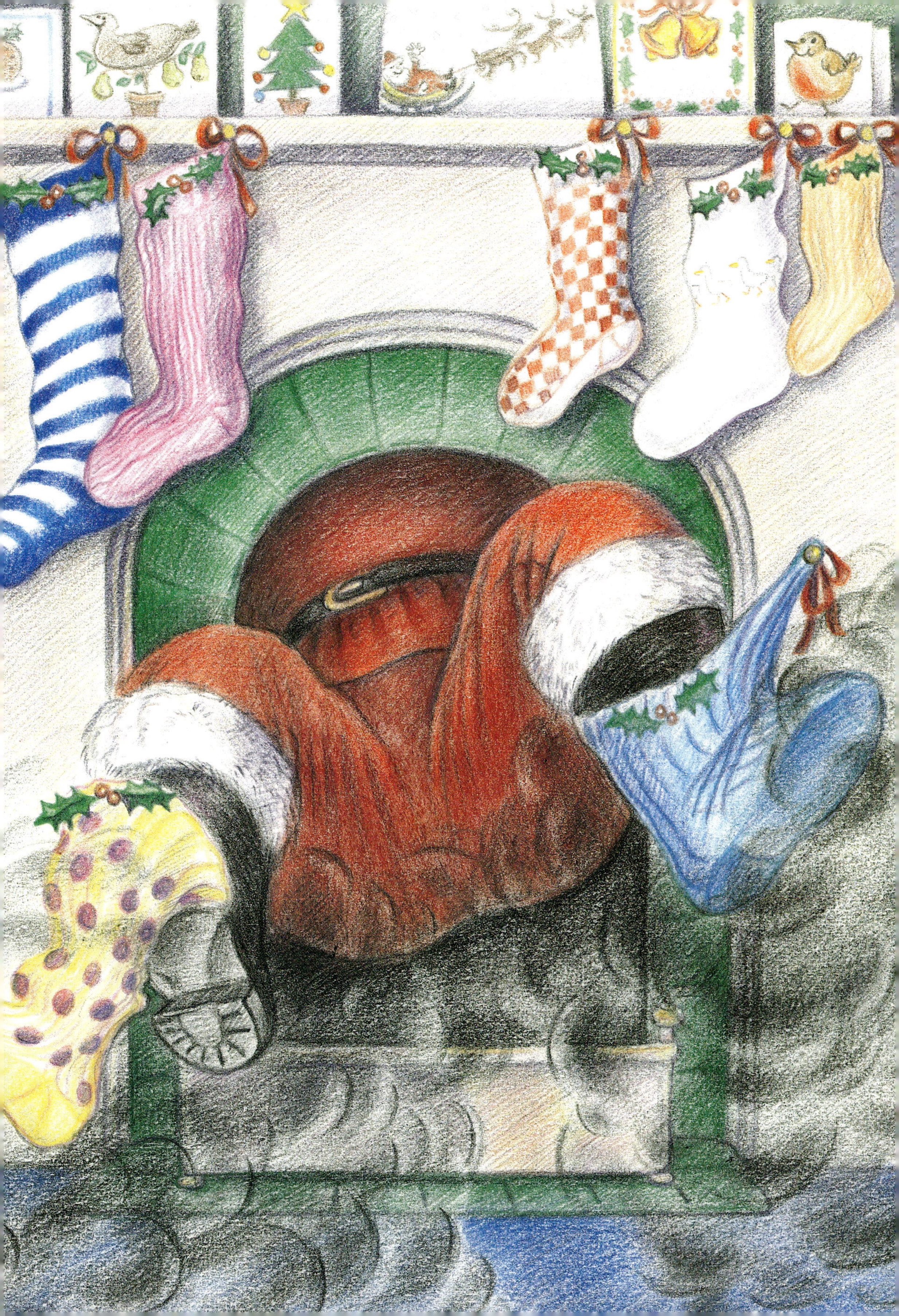

He was dressed all
  in fur from his head to his foot,
And his clothes were all tarnished with ashes
  and soot;
A bundle of toys he had flung on his back,
And he looked like a peddler just opening
  his pack.
His eyes how they twinkled! his dimples
  how merry!
His cheeks were like roses, his nose like a cherry;

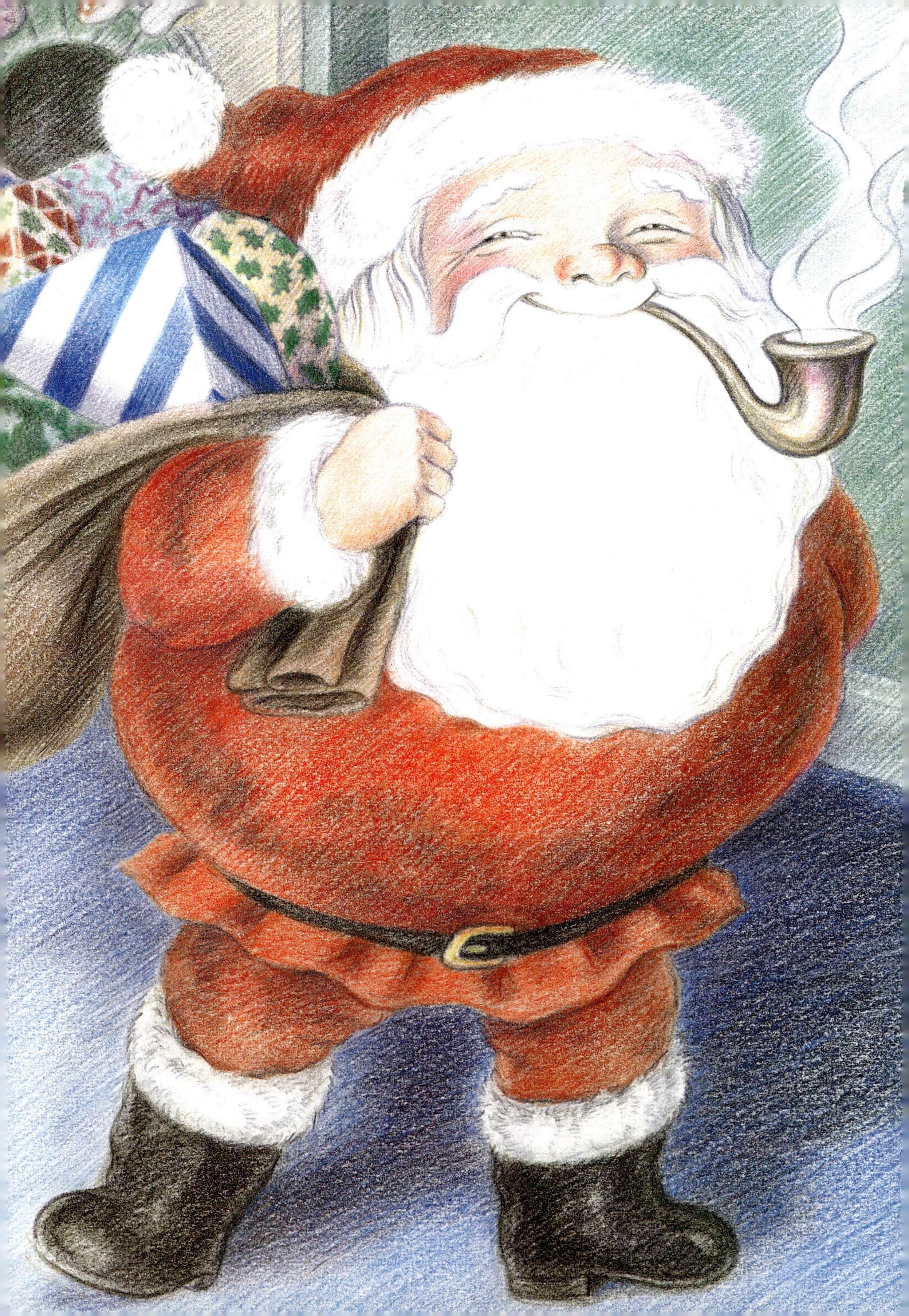

His droll little mouth was drawn up like a bow,
And the beard on his chin was as white as
 the snow.
The stump of a pipe he held tight in his teeth,
And the smoke it encircled his head like
 a wreath.
He had a broad face and a little round belly
That shook, when he laughed, like a bowl
 full of jelly.

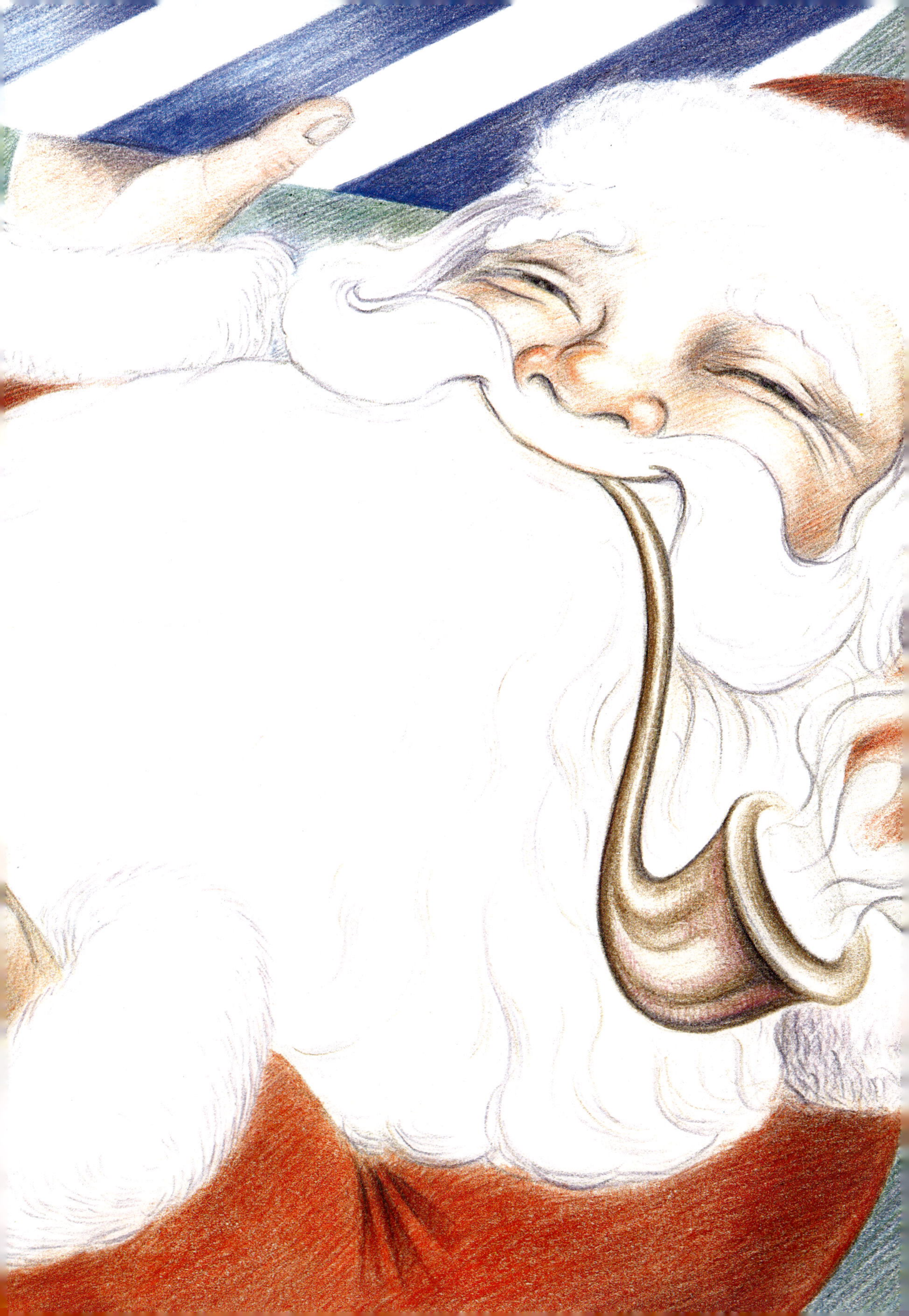

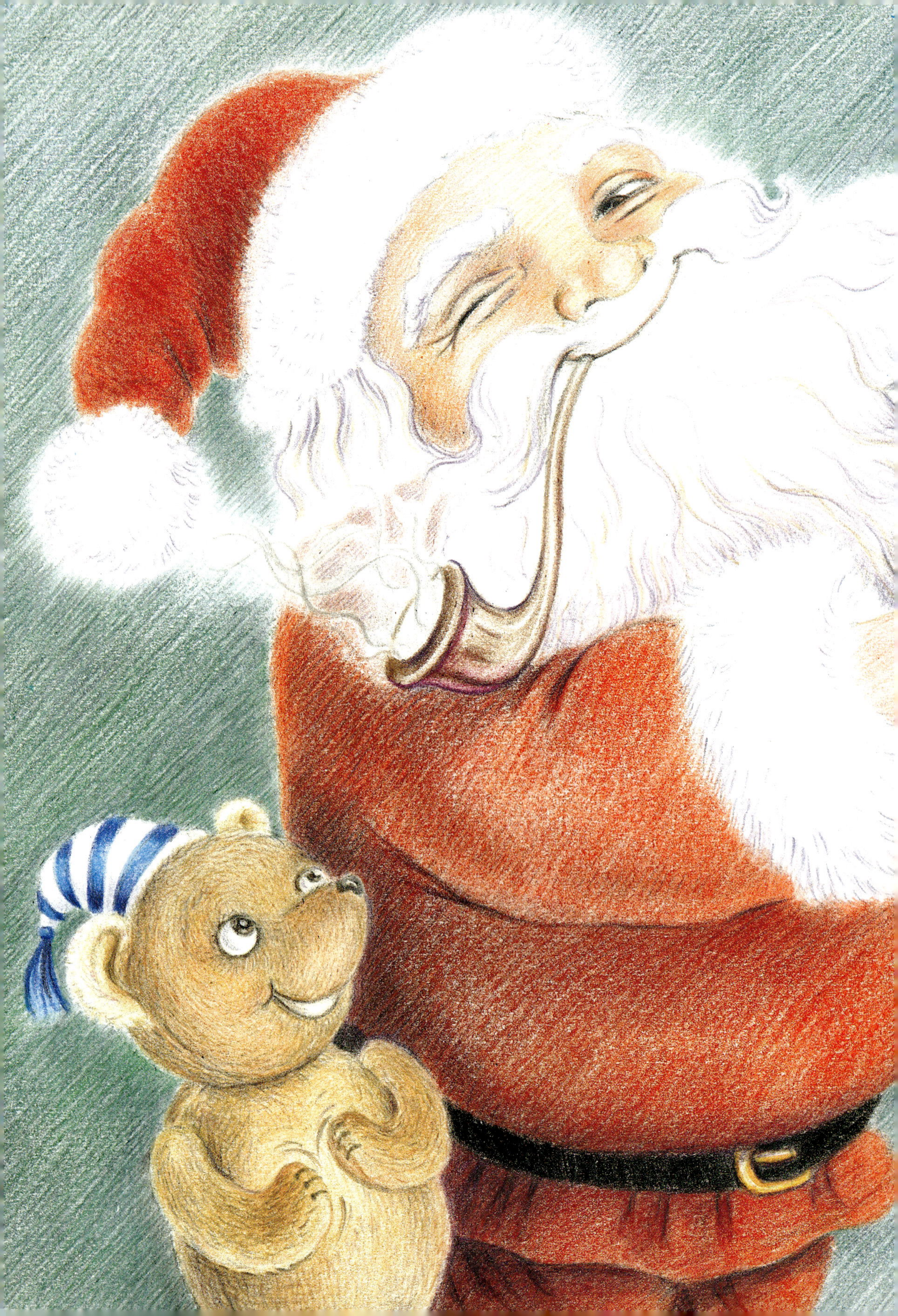

He was chubby and plump, a right jolly old elf,
And I laughed, when I saw him, in spite
  of myself.
A wink of his eye and a twist of his head
Soon gave me to know I had nothing to dread.
He spoke not a word, but went straight to
  his work,
And filled all the stockings; then turned with
  a jerk,

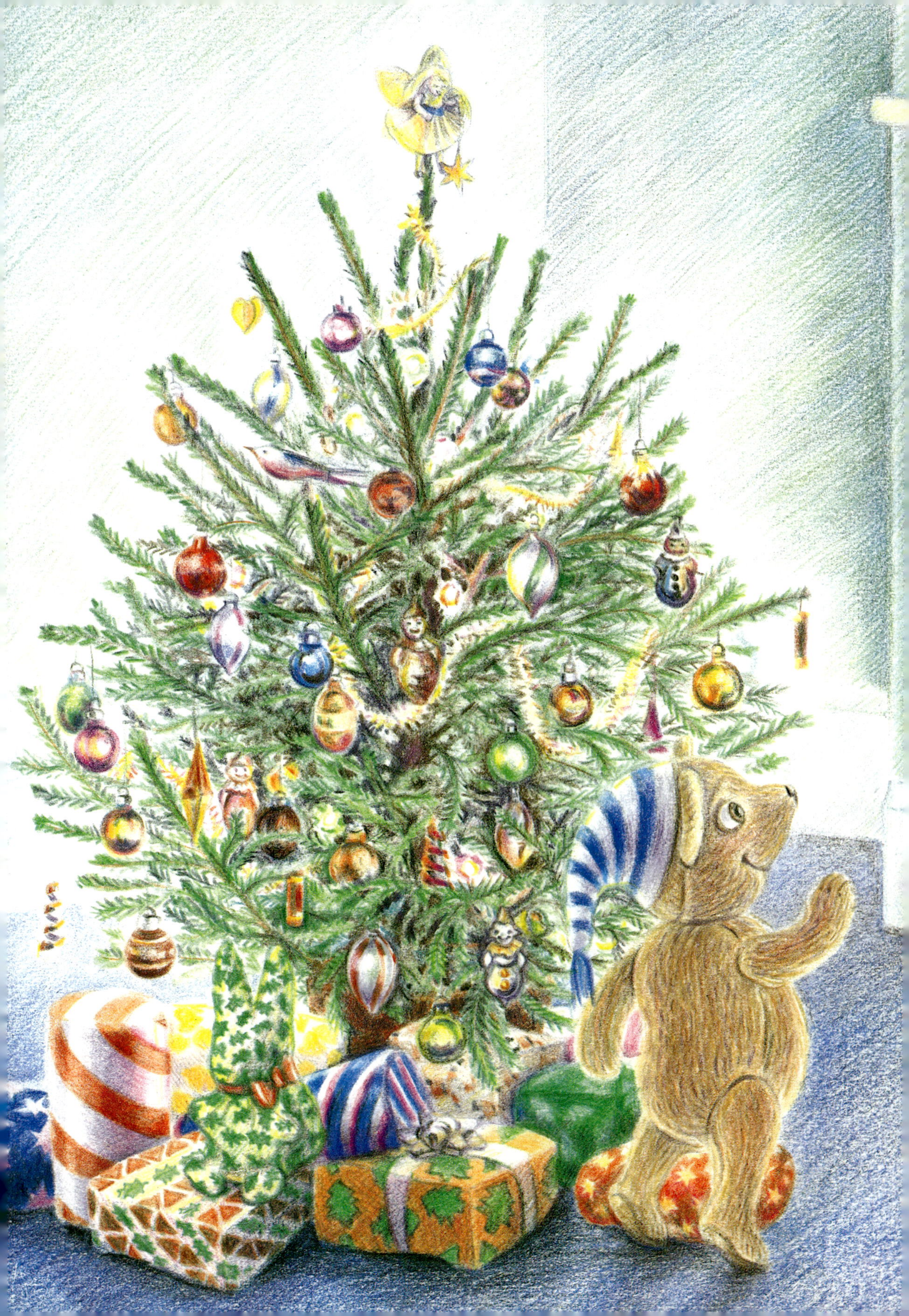

And laying his finger aside of his nose,
And giving a nod, up the chimney he rose.

He sprang to his sleigh, to his team gave
   a whistle,
And away they all flew like the down of
   a thistle;
But I heard him exclaim, ere he drove out
   of sight,
"Happy Christmas to all,
And to all a good-night!"

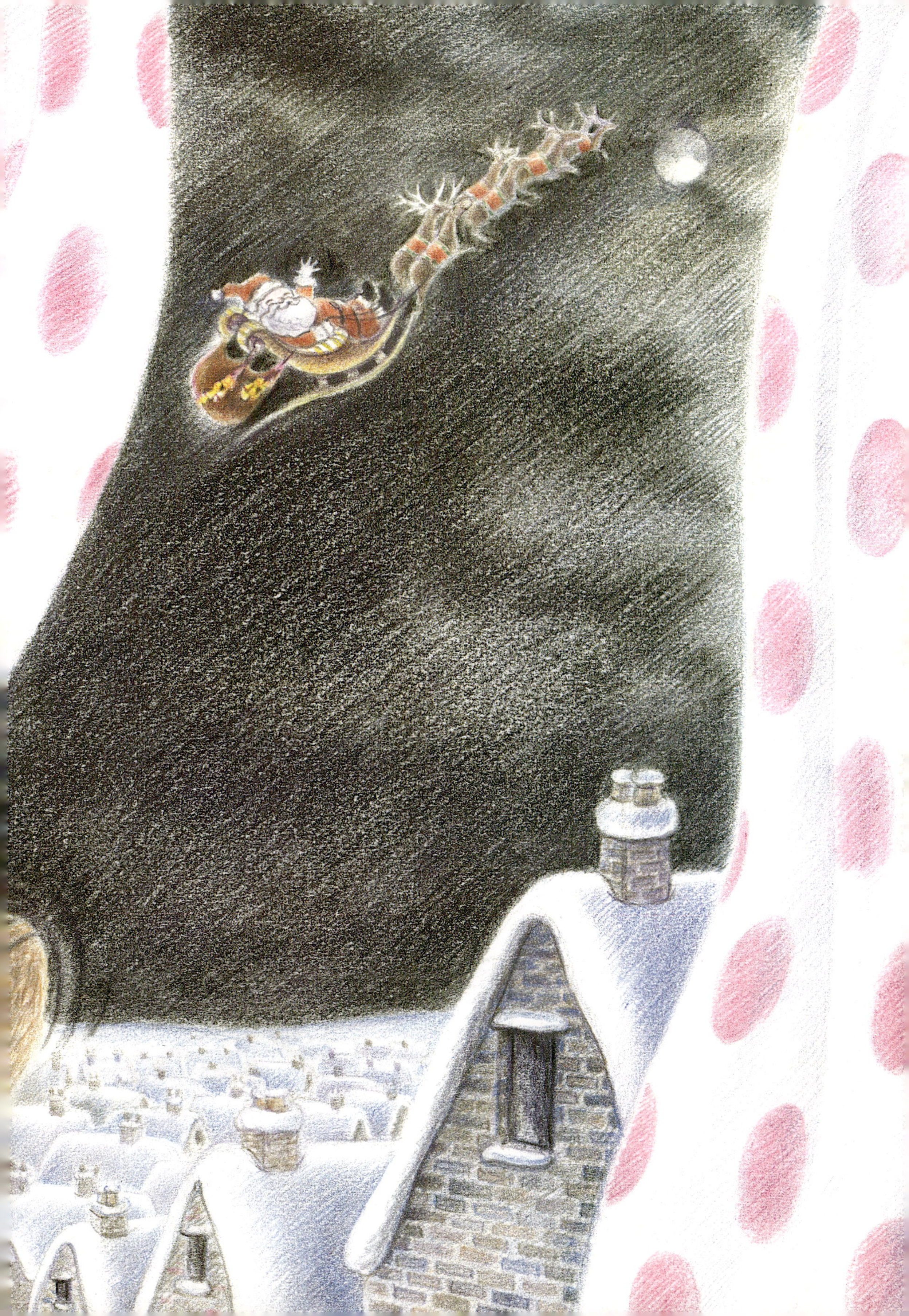

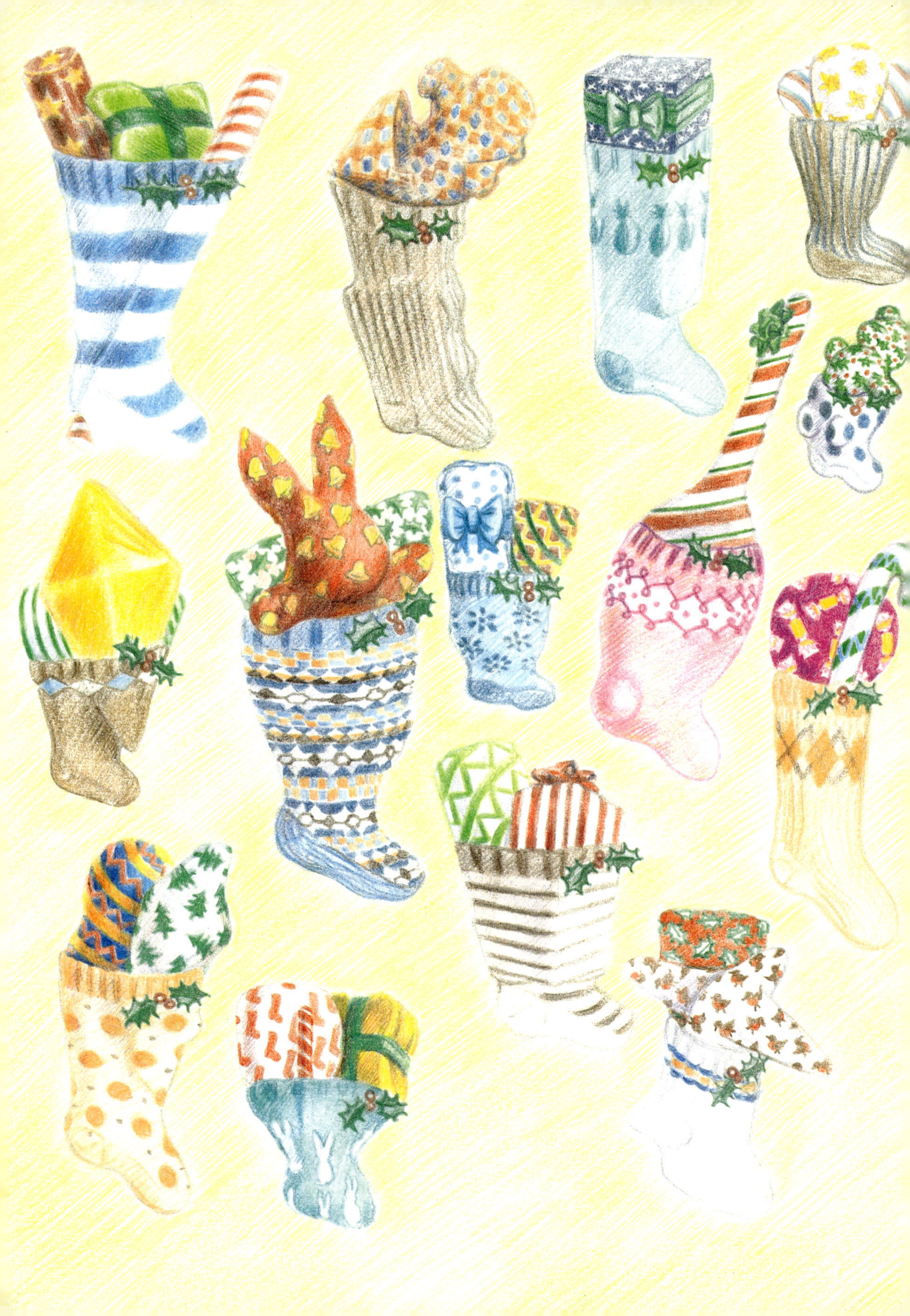

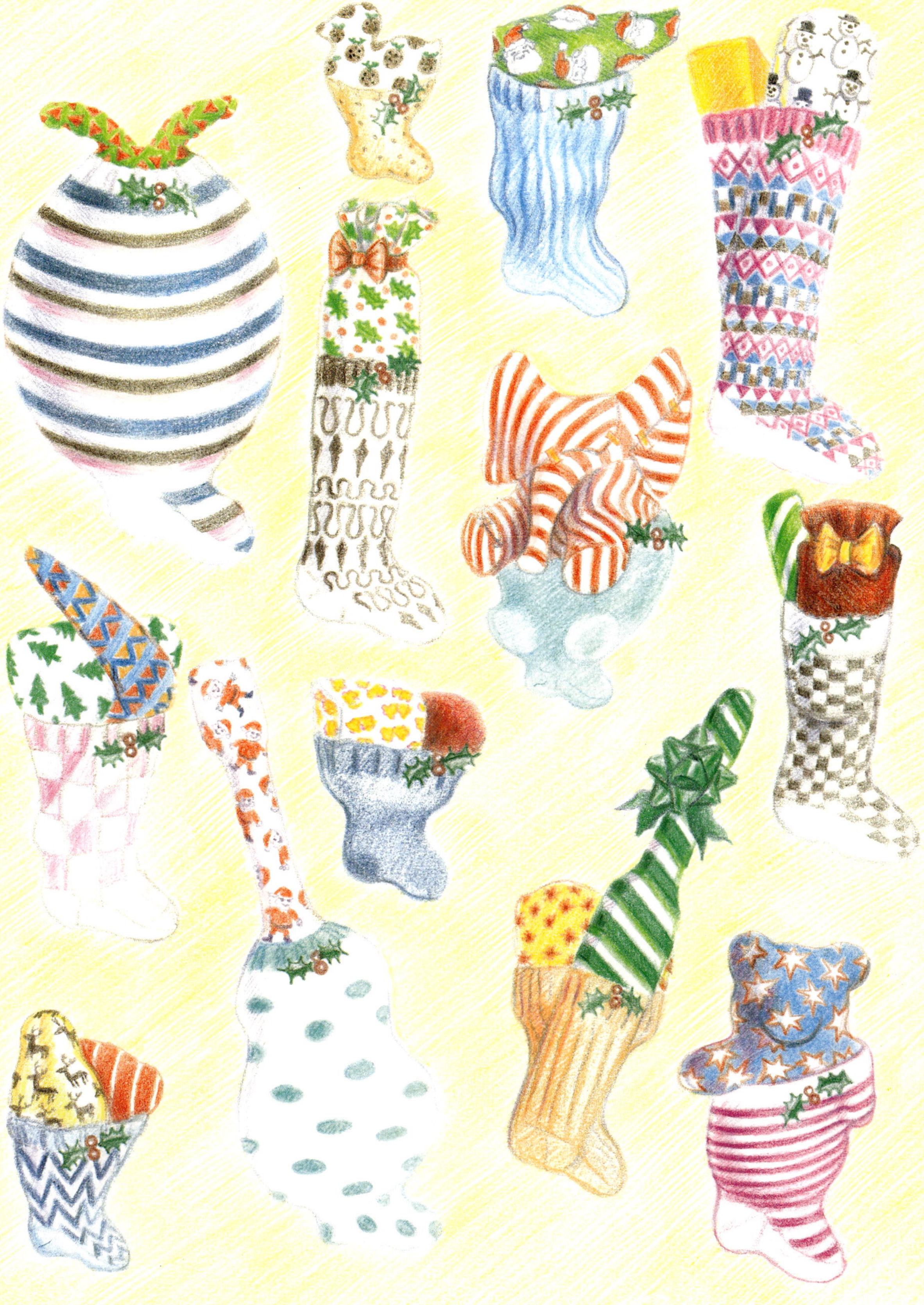

CLEMENT CLARKE MOORE was born in New York City in 1779. The son of a minister, he taught at New York's Diocesan Seminary and published political tracts, a Hebraic dictionary, and poetry. He wrote "A Visit from St. Nicholas" as a Christmas present for his daughter. His vision of the man now commonly known as Santa Claus was based in part on a local handyman who wore a red parka and often gave away sugarplums to children.